Betty Bailey

CHRISTMAS
LOVE

CHRISTMAS LOVE

CANDY CHAND

ILLUSTRATIONS BY JULIE OLSON

GIBBS SMITH

TO ENRICH AND INSPIRE HUMANKIND

Salt Lake City | Charleston | Santa Fe | Santa Barbara

12 11 10 09 08   10 9 8 7 6 5 4 3 2 1

First Gibbs Smith publication 2008

Text © 2005 Candy Chand

Illustrations © 2008 Julie Olson

Text previously published by permission of author in *Clarity Magazine*, 1999;
Heartwarmers.com, 2000; *Chicken Soup for the Christian Family's Soul*, 2000.

Published by
Gibbs Smith, Publisher
P.O. Box 667
Layton, Utah 84041

Orders: 1.800.835.4993
www.gibbs-smith.com

Designed by Dawn DeVries Sokol
Printed and bound in China

Library of Congress Cataloging-in-Publication Data

Chand, Candy.
  Christmas love : a true story of a holiday miracle / Candy Chand ;
illustrations by Julie Olson. — 1st ed.
     p. cm.
  ISBN-13: 978-1-4236-0276-7
  ISBN-10: 1-4236-0276-5
  1. Christmas. 2. Love—Religious aspects—Christianity. I. Olson, Julie,
1976- II. Title.
  BV45.C525 2008
  232.92—dc22
                        2008000722

TO NICHOLAS

Each December, I vow to make Christmas a
calm and peaceful experience.

One particular year, despite my good intentions, chaos prevailed. I had cut back on nonessential obligations—extensive card writing, endless baking, decorating, and, yes, even the all-American pastime: overspending. Yet, still, I found myself exhausted, unable to appreciate the precious family moments, and, of course, the true meaning of Christmas.

My son, Nicholas, was in kindergarten that year. It was an exciting season for a six-year-old, filled with hopes, dreams, and laughter. For weeks, he'd been memorizing songs for his school's "Winter Pageant." I didn't have the heart to tell him I'd be working the night of the production.

Winter Pageant

Come join us for a special night of song!

Thursday, 7:00 pm
in the Pleasantown School Auditorium

All parents, siblings and grandparents
are welcome to attend. General seating
only. Please arrive 15 minutes early and
send your children to their classrooms to
line up. Cameras and video recordings
are permitted along perimeters of the
auditorium only. See you Thursday!

Jingle Bells

Unwilling to miss his shining moment,
I spoke with his teacher. She assured me
there would be a dress rehearsal the
morning of the presentation. All parents
unable to attend that evening were welcome
to come then. Fortunately, Nicholas seemed
happy with the compromise.

So, just as I promised, on the morning of the dress rehearsal, I filed in ten minutes early, found a spot on the cafeteria floor, and sat down. Around the room, I saw several other parents searching for a place to sit.

As I waited, the students were led into the room. Each class, accompanied by their teacher, sat cross-legged on the floor. Then, one by one, each group rose to perform its song.

Because the public school system had long stopped referring to the holiday as "Christmas," I didn't expect anything other than fun, commercial entertainment—songs of reindeer, Santa Claus, snowflakes, and good cheer.

The melodies were amusing, cute, and light-hearted, but nowhere to be found was even the hint of an innocent babe, a manger, or Christ's sacred gift of hope and joy.

So, when my son's class rose to sing "Christmas Love," I was slightly taken aback by its bold title. Nicholas was aglow, as were his classmates, all adorned in fuzzy mittens, sweaters, and bright snowcaps upon their heads. Those in the front row—center stage—held up large letters, one by one, to spell out the title of the song.

As the class sang "C is for Christmas,"
a child held up the letter "C." Then "H
is for Happy," and on and on, until the
children presented the complete message,
"Christmas Love."

The performance was going smoothly until, suddenly, we noticed her—a small, quiet girl in the front row, holding the letter "M" upside down.

She was unaware that, reversed, her letter "M" appeared as a "W." Fidgeting from side to side, she soon moved entirely away from her mark.

The audience of 1st through 6th graders snickered at the little one's mistake. But in her innocence, she had no idea they were laughing at her as she stood tall, proudly holding her "W."

One can only imagine the difficulty in calming an audience of young, giggling students. Although many teachers tried to shush the children, the laughter continued until the last letter was raised and we all saw it together. A hush came over the audience and eyes began to widen.

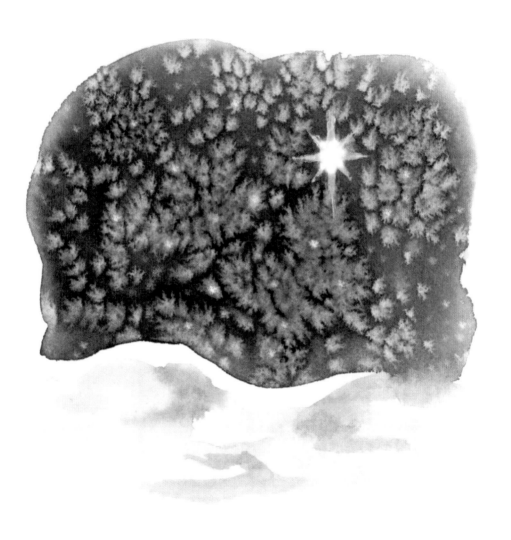

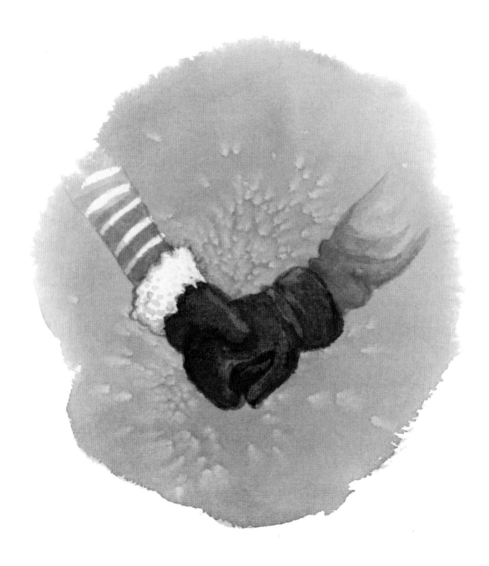

In that instant, we understood—the reason we were there, why we celebrated the holiday in the first place, why even in the chaos there was a purpose for our festivities.

For when the last letter was held high, the message read loud and clear:

And, I believe, He still is.